THE DISCOVERY HAGGADAH

Rabbi Kerry M. Olitzky
Rabbi Ronald H. Isaacs

Illustrated by Rachel Nachmani

*Dedicated to those to whom we will continue to
tell the story of our Exodus year after year, with
the prayer that they will continue to tell the story
to their children and grandchildren, as well:*

Emelia ("Mimi") Abigail Lebeau
Caleb Benjamin Lebeau

—RHI

Akiva Menachem Olitzky
Aliza Shoshana Olitzky
Miryam Tzipora Olitzky
Cayla Penina Olitzky

—KMO

Published by the United Synagogue of Conservative Judaism

ISBN 978-0-9834535-5-0

PROJECT MANAGEMENT BY DORRIE BERKOWITZ
ART DIRECTION BY JOSEF TOCKER
ILLUSTRATION BY RACHEL NACHMANI rach.nach1@gmail.com
DESIGN AND COMPOSITION BY MILES B. COHEN

PRINTED IN CANADA

CONTENTS

A Note for Parents and Teachers

This haggadah leads you on a discovery to find the Pesach seder that is most meaningful for your students or family. The essential seder service is contained in this haggadah and is written in a voice easily understood by growing-up families and children.

Each section and subsection is introduced by

 explaining the reason behind the specific section, and

 offering simple, direct instructions for completing that part of the seder.

The traditional text with explanation is included. The activities for discovery follow. Try them out and add your own. They are particularly good for model sedarim in schools. But be careful. Don't try to do them all at once. Leave some for your sedarim in years to come.

Here is the key to the activity icons:

Questions

Innovations

Imagination

Songs

Games to Play

Curiosities

The beauty of the haggadah is that it contains the hopes and aspirations—and even the fears—of each generation. It is truly a sacred living text. We pray that the haggadah is part of the fabric of your family and students as it is of our own.

Rabbi Kerry M. Olitzky
Rabbi Ronald H. Isaacs
Passover 5773

בְּדִיקַת חָמֵץ | B'dikat Chametz
Getting Ready for Pesach

After you have done your Pesach spring cleaning, on the night before Pesach collect all the remaining chametz in your home. Search it out with candle, feather, and spoon. Set it aside until morning, when we burn it or otherwise fully dispose of it (*bi·ur chametz*). Before the search, recite the text from Exodus and the blessing.

זָכוֹר אֶת־הַיּוֹם הַזֶּה אֲשֶׁר יְצָאתֶם מִמִּצְרַיִם מִבֵּית עֲבָדִים,
כִּי בְּחֹזֶק יָד הוֹצִיא יי אֶתְכֶם מִזֶּה, וְלֹא יֵאָכֵל חָמֵץ.

Remember this day as the day you left Egypt, from the house of slavery. It was with a mighty hand that Adonai led you out. No chametz should be eaten.

Exodus 13:3

בָּרוּךְ אַתָּה יי   Barukh atah adonai

אֱלֹהֵינוּ מֶלֶךְ הָעוֹלָם,   eloheinu melekh ha·olam,

אֲשֶׁר קִדְּשָׁנוּ בְּמִצְוֹתָיו,   asher kid'shanu b'mitz·votav

וְצִוָּנוּ עַל בִּעוּר חָמֵץ.   v'tzivanu al bi·ur chametz.

Praised are You, Adonai our God, Guide of the Universe, who gave us the special gift of mitzvot and instructed us to remove chametz from our homes.

In the morning, after the chametz has been disposed of, say:

I am ready to welcome the Festival of Matzot into our home. May it bring us close to freedom and peace.

Ma·ot chitim: Collect tzedakah called "wheat money" to help buy Passover foods for Jews who cannot afford Passover foods. You can donate your chametz to non-Jews who are hungry.

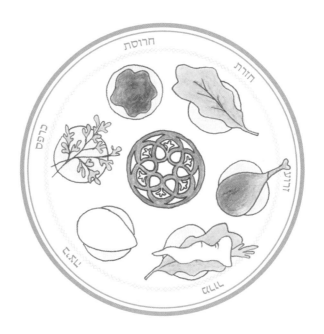

Seder Symbols

זְרוֹעַ | **Z'roa**

Symbol of the Pesach offering. Usually a roasted bone (or a boiled beet for vegetarians).

כַּרְפַּס | **Karpas**

Symbol of spring. A vegetable, usually parsley or other green vegetable.

מָרוֹר | **Maror**

Symbol of the bitterness of slave life. Bitter vegetable, usually horseradish or romaine lettuce.

בֵּיצָה | **Beitzah**

Symbol of the ancient festival offering. A roasted egg (or an avocado seed for vegetarians).

חֲרֹסֶת | **Charoset**

Symbol of mortar. A mixture usually including chopped apples, chopped nuts, wine, and spices.

חֲזֶרֶת | **Chazeret**

An additional variety of bitter vegetable, usually romaine lettuce.

מַצָּה | **Matzah**

Symbol of slavery, poverty, and the Exodus. Three unbroken pieces of matzah.

The Seder (Order)
of the Seder

The seder program consists of fourteen different ceremonies. To make it easier to remember, the ceremonial names are sung to a special melody . . . Kadesh, Urchatz . . .

1
KADESH
  Special and Holy

2
UR·CHATZ
  Washing

3
KARPAS
  Green Things

4
YACHATZ
  Break It in the Middle

5
MAGID
  The Telling and Retelling

6
ROCH·TZAH
  Cleansing

מוֹצִיא מַצָּה

7
MOTZI MATZAH
Eating "Matzah Bread"

מָרוֹר

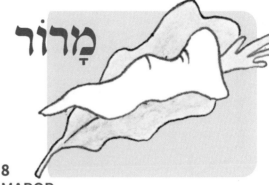

8
MAROR
Bitter Vegetable

כּוֹרֵךְ

9
KOREKH
Hillel's Sandwich

שֻׁלְחָן עוֹרֵךְ

10
SHULCHAN OREKH
The Meal Is Served

צָפוּן

11
TZAFUN
The Hidden Afikoman

בָּרֵךְ

12
BAREKH
Giving Thanks

הַלֵּל

13
HALLEL
Songs of Praise

נִרְצָה

14
NIR·TZAH
Acceptance

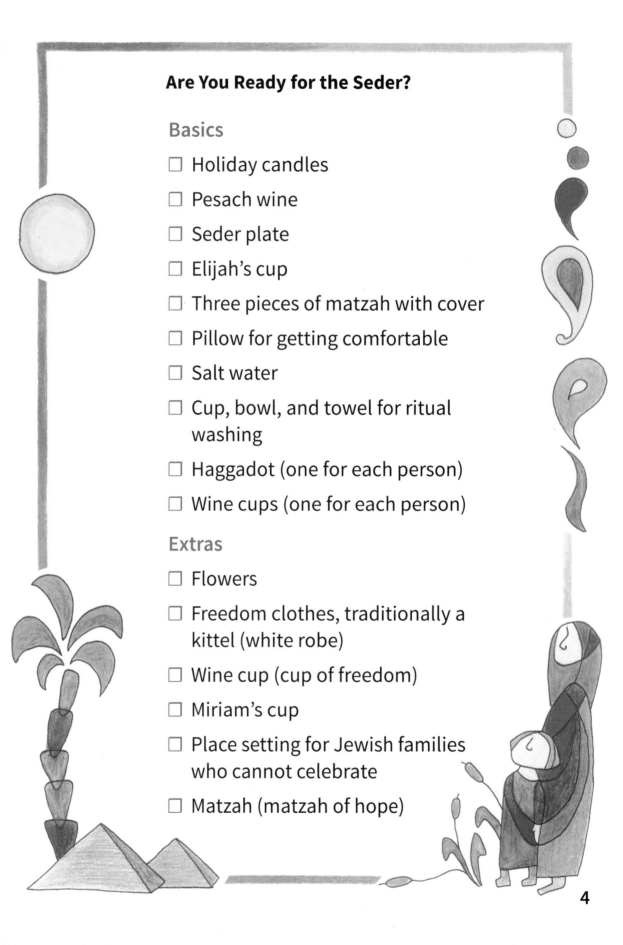

Are You Ready for the Seder?

Basics

- ☐ Holiday candles
- ☐ Pesach wine
- ☐ Seder plate
- ☐ Elijah's cup
- ☐ Three pieces of matzah with cover
- ☐ Pillow for getting comfortable
- ☐ Salt water
- ☐ Cup, bowl, and towel for ritual washing
- ☐ Haggadot (one for each person)
- ☐ Wine cups (one for each person)

Extras

- ☐ Flowers
- ☐ Freedom clothes, traditionally a kittel (white robe)
- ☐ Wine cup (cup of freedom)
- ☐ Miriam's cup
- ☐ Place setting for Jewish families who cannot celebrate
- ☐ Matzah (matzah of hope)

The
Seder

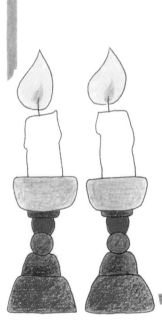

קַדֵּשׁ | Kadesh
Special and Holy

WHY Just as on every festival and every Shabbat, we mark the specialness of the day by saying a special blessing over a cup of wine. The Kiddush is particularly important on Pesach because each time we say it we are reminded of *y'tzi·at Mitzrayim*—the Exodus from Egypt. On our way to Canaan (now called Israel), we received the Torah and slowly but surely became the Jewish people. We drink four cups during the seder, one for each promise God made to our Israelite ancestors in Egypt. This one is for "I will free you from the burden of [working as a slave for] the Egyptians" (Exodus 6:6).

HOW TO Fill your glass with wine (or grape juice). You'll have to do this four times during the seder. It's OK to fill it full and let it spill over a little, since our hearts are filled up with happiness about leaving slavery behind in Egypt. Drink the wine after you have said all the blessings (ending on p. 8). And don't forget to get comfortable. Special table manners tonight—you're free to sit in a way that's most comfortable for you.

Kos Rishonah | כּוֹס רִאשׁוֹנָה
The First Cup

הִנְנִי מוּכָן וּמְזֻמָּן   Hin'ni mukhan umzuman

לְקַיֵּם מִצְוַת כּוֹס רִאשׁוֹנָה.   l'kayem mitz·vat kos rishonah.

I am ready to fulfill the mitzvah of drinking the first cup of wine.

בָּרוּךְ אַתָּה יי   Barukh atah adonai

אֱלֹהֵינוּ מֶלֶךְ הָעוֹלָם,   eloheinu melekh ha·olam,

בּוֹרֵא פְּרִי הַגָּפֶן.   borei p'ri hagafen.

Praised are You, Adonai our God, Guide of the Universe,
who creates fruit that grows on the vine.

On Shabbat add the words in brackets.

בָּרוּךְ אַתָּה יי אֱלֹהֵינוּ מֶלֶךְ הָעוֹלָם, אֲשֶׁר בָּחַר בָּנוּ מִכָּל־עָם,
וְרוֹמְמָנוּ מִכָּל־לָשׁוֹן, וְקִדְּשָׁנוּ בְּמִצְוֹתָיו, וַתִּתֶּן־לָנוּ יי אֱלֹהֵינוּ
בְּאַהֲבָה [שַׁבָּתוֹת לִמְנוּחָה וּ] מוֹעֲדִים לְשִׂמְחָה, חַגִּים וּזְמַנִּים
לְשָׂשׂוֹן, אֶת־יוֹם [הַשַּׁבָּת הַזֶּה וְאֶת־יוֹם] חַג הַמַּצּוֹת הַזֶּה
זְמַן חֵרוּתֵנוּ, [בְּאַהֲבָה] מִקְרָא קֹדֶשׁ, זֵכֶר לִיצִיאַת מִצְרָיִם.
כִּי בָנוּ בָחַרְתָּ וְאוֹתָנוּ קִדַּשְׁתָּ מִכָּל־הָעַמִּים, [וְשַׁבָּת] וּמוֹעֲדֵי
קָדְשְׁךָ [בְּאַהֲבָה וּבְרָצוֹן] בְּשִׂמְחָה וּבְשָׂשׂוֹן הִנְחַלְתָּנוּ.
בָּרוּךְ אַתָּה יי, מְקַדֵּשׁ [הַשַּׁבָּת וְ] יִשְׂרָאֵל וְהַזְּמַנִּים.

Praised are You, Adonai our God, Guide of the Universe, who
chose us from among the peoples by giving us the special gift
of mitzvot. Out of love, You have given us happy holidays to
celebrate, including [this Shabbat and] this terrific Pesach, our
time of freedom, a special and holy time to help us remember
y'tzi·at Mitzrayim, the Exodus from Egypt. You have chosen us,
separating us from other peoples by [Shabbat and] special festivals
which we happily celebrate. Praised are You, Adonai, who makes
special [the holy Shabbat] and the people Israel and its festivals.

Don't drink yet. Continue on the next page.

If the seder falls on Saturday night, add the next two sections.

בָּרוּךְ אַתָּה יי אֱלֹהֵינוּ מֶלֶךְ הָעוֹלָם, בּוֹרֵא מְאוֹרֵי הָאֵשׁ.

Praised are You, Adonai our God, Guide of the Universe, creator of light.

בָּרוּךְ אַתָּה יי אֱלֹהֵינוּ מֶלֶךְ הָעוֹלָם, הַמַּבְדִּיל בֵּין קֹדֶשׁ
לְחֹל בֵּין אוֹר לְחֹשֶׁךְ, בֵּין יִשְׂרָאֵל לָעַמִּים, בֵּין יוֹם הַשְּׁבִיעִי
לְשֵׁשֶׁת יְמֵי הַמַּעֲשֶׂה. בֵּין קְדֻשַּׁת שַׁבָּת לִקְדֻשַּׁת יוֹם טוֹב
הִבְדַּלְתָּ, וְאֶת־יוֹם הַשְּׁבִיעִי מִשֵּׁשֶׁת יְמֵי הַמַּעֲשֶׂה קִדַּשְׁתָּ,
הִבְדַּלְתָּ וְקִדַּשְׁתָּ אֶת־עַמְּךָ יִשְׂרָאֵל בִּקְדֻשָּׁתֶךָ.
בָּרוּךְ אַתָּה יי, הַמַּבְדִּיל בֵּין קֹדֶשׁ לְקֹדֶשׁ.

Praised are You, Adonai our God, Guide of the Universe, who separates the holy from the everyday, light from darkness, Israel from the nations, and Shabbat from the six days of creation. We praise You, Adonai, who separates the holiness of Shabbat from the holiness of the festivals.

On all days continue here.

בָּרוּךְ אַתָּה יי אֱלֹהֵינוּ מֶלֶךְ הָעוֹלָם,
שֶׁהֶחֱיָנוּ וְקִיְּמָנוּ וְהִגִּיעָנוּ לַזְּמַן הַזֶּה.

Praised are You, Adonai our God, Guide of the Universe, who has kept us alive and sustained us so that we can celebrate this special time.

Drink the wine.

Kiddush, kadesh, and *kadosh* all come from the Hebrew word meaning "holy" or "special." What does the word "holy" mean to you? Talk about times when you felt holy. Describe an object in your home which you think is holy.

The first line of the Kiddush describes God's choosing us to be special people. In what way do you feel special? Talk about a time when someone chose you to do something special.

Why do you think we recline on the left side?

The name "Pesach" probably comes from the Hebrew word *pasach,* meaning "to pass over." Ask everyone at your seder, in turn, to tell the group about something they would not want to pass over.

Here are some things that we cannot "pass over" on Pesach:
a. Concern for those who are not free
b. Remembering our loved ones
c. Concern for the environment
d. Feeding the hungry

Set aside an extra cup of wine (in addition to the one already prepared for Elijah the Prophet). Leave this cup empty. Tell everyone at the seder that this cup is to honor all those who are not free to join your Passover seder.

Go outside and look at the full moon. Why does Passover begin with a full moon?

Reserve an extra chair and complete place setting for all Jews who are still "slaves." Place a pillow on the chair as a symbol of hope for a time when they will be at ease.

German Jews often use white wine instead of red so that it is not mistaken for blood.

In the past, Jews began their sedarim by opening the door and inviting all who were hungry to come and eat. As persecutions of the Jews increased, such announcements became dangerous and the "open door" policy was used to make sure no one was listening at the door.

Yemenite Jews sprinkle their clothing with incense before the seder to make the night even more special. Jews from the Caucasus Mountains used to wear loose-fitting, tunic-like garments that they called "liberty clothes."

וּרְחַץ | Ur·chatz
Washing

WHY Since the seder is so special, we make a big deal out of washing our hands and getting ready. We want to make them ritually clean because we are going to do holy things.

HOW TO Use a pitcher or cup and pour water over each hand, one at a time. No need to say the blessing for washing hands yet. We'll save that for later, before the meal.

Passover Word Search. What Passover words can you find in the word search below? Give yourself one point for each correct answer. See who can find the most words most quickly at the seder.

M	V	K	E	N	I
A	S	I	G	P	O
T	T	D	Y	R	C
Z	J	L	P	B	E
A	W	A	T	E	R
H	B	S	A	L	T

(Answers on page 73.)

Why do you think at this point we wash our hands without a blessing?

Some say that we wash our hands because in ancient times it was a custom to do so before dipping things in liquids. Liquids were considered to pass on ritual impurity. Others say we do so because the ancient priests washed before approaching the Temple altar. Tonight, the table is transformed into a sacred altar.

כַּרְפַּס | Karpas
Green Things

WHY Spring is a special time of year. Everything seems to come alive again after being dormant all winter. It is also the rebirth of the Jewish people. But all was not perfect. There were lots of salty tears when we were slaves. That's why we dip greens into salt water—to mix our sadness with the hope that spring brings to life.

HOW TO Take your green vegetable, usually parsley, and dip it in salt water. (This is your first dipping; remember that when you ask the Four Questions.) Then eat it, but say the blessing first. Yes, you can slouch for this one too.

בָּרוּךְ אַתָּה יי   Barukh atah adonai

אֱלֹהֵינוּ מֶלֶךְ הָעוֹלָם,   eloheinu melekh ha·olam,

בּוֹרֵא פְּרִי הָאֲדָמָה.   borei p'ri ha·adamah.

Praised are You, Adonai our God, Guide of the Universe, who creates things that grow in the ground.

Serve platefuls of karpas appetizer (celery, carrots, parsley, radishes) along with some dip so that those who are really hungry can eat something before the meal.

Again chant the seder ("order") of the seder. But this time, stop at the step in the seder just about to be celebrated. For example, when you reach the karpas part of the seder, before actually doing the karpas ritual, chant up to "Karpas." This is like an announcement for the next step in the seder. Continue this rechanting of the steps each time you come to a new section throughout the seder.

Rabbi Yehudah said: "Someone who goes out in the month of Nisan and sees the trees in bloom should recite the blessing: 'Praised are You, Adonai, who has not left the world lacking in anything and has created in it good trees to give pleasure to humankind'" (Babylonian Talmud, Berakhot 43b). Go outside, find a new spring blossom, and recite this blessing!

People wonder whether parsley is the only vegetable to use for karpas. Many people use parsley because it is fresh and green, like spring. But other tasty vegetables may be used, such as celery and radishes. Some people even use potatoes.

Greeks and Romans would often dip hors d'oeuvres before they ate a big banquet meal.

יַחַץ | Yachatz
Break It in the Middle

WHY There are lots of reasons why we stack three pieces of matzah and then break the middle one. Since we use two loaves of challah for Shabbat and festivals (one loaf representing the ordinary bread of every day and the extra one for the extra pre-Shabbat portion of heavenly manna), we add a third to remind us that matzah is the bread of affliction. The three pieces also remind us that as Jews we are all in this together whether our ancestors were Kohanim (priests), Levites (assistant priests), or Israelites (just plain folks). We break bread—the middle matzah—to be hospitable to everyone we have invited to share the seder with us. We also do it to emphasize how little we had to eat as slaves, but in an unusual sort of way this shared matzah experience binds us all together as a people.

The afikoman is wrapped up in much the same way as the Israelites wrapped their baking tools when they quickly left Egypt.

HOW TO Take the three pieces of matzah you have set aside for the seder. Break the middle matzah into two pieces. Let someone hide the larger piece as the afikoman. Don't look! We'll search for it later. Then put back the other broken piece between the two unbroken pieces.

 In some European families, when the leader is not looking, the children hide the afikoman and ransom it later.

 Moroccan Jews have a tradition of tossing the afikoman into the sea (prior to a voyage) in order to calm the seas and prevent storms (based on Psalm 54:9: "God has saved me from all trouble").

Yemenite tradition suggests that the name "afikoman" came from these words:

אֱגוֹזִים	nuts
פֵּרוֹת	fruit
יַיִן	wine
קְלָיוֹת	roasted things
וּבָשָׂר	and meat
מַיִם	water
נֵרְדְּ	spikenard (fragrant herb)

אֲפִיקוֹמָן | Afikoman

If you could invite anyone to your seder to join you in this meal, who would you invite? Why?

Add one more matzah to the pile. Call it a matzah of hope. Lift it and set it aside as a symbol for all Jews throughout the world who are not able to celebrate a Passover seder in the way they would like. You may also want to talk a little about what your family might be able to do to help them celebrate Passover.

Sephardic Jews place the wrapped afikoman in a bag, which is then thrown over the shoulder and carried around the seder table. This makes them feel like they are rushing out of Egypt like our ancestors did during the Exodus.

Jewish mystics (known as Kabbalists) break the middle matzah into the shape of the Hebrew letters *dalet* and *vav,* the fourth and sixth letters of the alphabet. According to gematria, this makes a total of 10, equaling the number of *sefirot,* or levels of mystical spheres, in the universe. See if you can do it.

In some communities there used to be a custom of inscribing the three matzot with the words Kohen, Levi, and Israelite. Other communities marked them with the first three letters of the Hebrew alphabet.

מַגִּיד | Magid
The Telling and Retelling

WHY This begins the telling and retelling of the story of how the Israelites were slaves in Egypt and eventually were freed by God through the leadership of Moses. The whole saga is symbolized by the matzah. When we look at it, we try to remember what it was like to have been slaves in Egypt, because in a funny sort of way, we were all there. We invite others to share in the seder meal and to hear the story of our ancestors. We remember what it was like to be strangers in a strange land, and so we invite guests to our table. We begin with *Ha lachma anya* because not all of our people are free even today. Some are still forced to live like slaves.

HOW TO Uncover the matzah. Hold it up so that all can see it and then read *Ha lachma anya.* You may want to add your own prayer at this point in the seder for those of our brothers and sisters who may not be able to celebrate Passover.

הָא לַחְמָא עַנְיָא דִי אֲכָלוּ אַבְהָתָנָא בְּאַרְעָא דְמִצְרָיִם.
כָּל־דִכְפִין יֵיתֵי וְיֵכוֹל, כָּל־דִצְרִיךְ יֵיתֵי וְיִפְסַח.
הַשַּׁתָּא הָכָא, לְשָׁנָה הַבָּאָה בְּאַרְעָא דְיִשְׂרָאֵל.
הַשַּׁתָּא עַבְדֵי, לְשָׁנָה הַבָּאָה בְּנֵי חוֹרִין.

Ha lachma anya: This is the Bread of Poverty which our ancestors ate in the land of Egypt. Let all who are hungry come join us for the meal. Let all who are in need come and celebrate Pesach with us. Now we are here. May we be in the land of Israel next year. Now we are slaves. May we all be free next year.

Remove the seder plate or place it at the end of the table. This will help to stimulate everyone's curiosity. It can later be moved back to the center of the table.

Among Moroccan families, the middle matzah is broken into two pieces to resemble the Hebrew letter *hei*, standing for God. At the same time, everyone sings an Arabic song which recalls the miracle of the Red Sea. This *hei*-shaped matzah is then taken by each member of the family and held against their eyes as *Ha lachma anya* is recited.

Bukharan Jews stand up during the Magid section and walk around the seder table in a bent-over posture, as if they were still slaves.

מַה־נִּשְׁתַּנָּה | **Mah Nishtanah**
One Big Question, Four Big Answers

WHY Since the Magid section of the seder is the retelling of the Pesach story, it is natural to begin with an answer to the question: Why Pesach? The Four Questions really started as examples of questions that might be asked to begin the seder, but they quickly became favorites. And now everyone asks the same questions in pretty much the same way. The big question remains: Why is this night of the seder so different from all other nights?

HOW TO Anyone can ask the questions, but usually the youngest person at the seder reads *Mah nishtanah.* Read or sing or chant them one at a time, then take a deep breath and relax. Listen to the answers for a couple of hours. But re-cover the matzah and fill your cup a second time. You will want to get ready for what comes next.

מַה־נִּשְׁתַּנָּה הַלַּיְלָה הַזֶּה · מִכָּל־הַלֵּילוֹת!   Mah nishtanah halailah hazeh mikol haleilot!

How different is this night of seder from all other nights!

1 שֶׁבְּכָל־הַלֵּילוֹת אָנוּ אוֹכְלִין חָמֵץ וּמַצָּה, הַלַּיְלָה הַזֶּה כֻּלּוֹ מַצָּה.   Sheb'khol haleilot anu okh'lin chametz umatzah, halailah hazeh kulo matzah.

On all other nights, we eat either chametz or matzah.
Why do we only eat matzah tonight?

2 שֶׁבְּכָל־הַלֵּילוֹת אָנוּ אוֹכְלִין שְׁאָר יְרָקוֹת, הַלַּיְלָה הַזֶּה מָרוֹר.   Sheb'khol haleilot anu okh'lin sh'ar y'rakot, halailah hazeh maror.

On all other nights we (try to) eat all kinds of vegetables.
Why do we eat bitter vegetables tonight?

3 שֶׁבְּכָל־הַלֵּילוֹת אֵין אָנוּ מַטְבִּילִין אֲפִלּוּ פַּעַם אֶחָת, הַלַּיְלָה הַזֶּה שְׁתֵּי פְעָמִים.   Sheb'khol haleilot ein anu matbilin afilu pa·am echat, halailah hazeh sh'tei f'amim.

On all other nights we usually don't dip our vegetables at all.
Why do we dip our vegetables twice tonight?

4 שֶׁבְּכָל־הַלֵּילוֹת אָנוּ אוֹכְלִין בֵּין יוֹשְׁבִין וּבֵין מְסֻבִּין, הַלַּיְלָה הַזֶּה כֻּלָּנוּ מְסֻבִּין.   Sheb'khol haleilot anu okh'lin bein yosh'vin uvein m'subin, halailah hazeh kulanu m'subin.

On all other nights we eat either sitting straight or sitting in a relaxed position. Why do we eat sitting only in a relaxed position tonight?

What are some other questions that you might want to ask that are important to today's Jewish community? For example, why are people still starving? Why is there still fighting in the world?

At some Sephardic sedarim, the leader or one of the participants leaves the room after the Four Questions, then returns a few minutes later with a napkin containing the afikoman slung over a shoulder. Everyone at the table then asks: "Who are you?" The person who left the room answers: "A Jew." And the dialogue continues. Questions and answers are exchanged, such as: "Where do you come from?" "From Egypt." "What did you do there?" "I was a slave."

Why do we ask the same questions every year?
Why are the Four Questions not answered immediately?

(Answer on page 73.)

The Four Questions in our present-day haggadot are not the same as in those in really old haggadot. One question no longer in use was: On all other nights we eat our meat either boiled or roasted. Why on this night do we eat it roasted? (The roasted meat was a reminder of the roasted Pesach lamb that was sacrificed in the Temple.)

עֲבָדִים הָיִינוּ | **Avadim Hayinu**
We Were Slaves

WHY The rabbis have taught us that in order to fully appreciate the seder experience, we have to relive the life our ancestors lived in Egypt step by step, beginning with slavery and ending with freedom. Here we begin the story of our past by reminding ourselves that we were slaves. For the rabbis, slavery represented both a state of mind and a historical experience. God forcefully brought us out of physical Egypt and through divine nurturing got it out of our heads too. Even if we already know the story, we tell it again and again. It's all part of being Jewish.

עֲבָדִים הָיִינוּ לְפַרְעֹה בְּמִצְרָיִם. וַיּוֹצִיאֵנוּ יי אֱלֹהֵינוּ מִשָּׁם,
בְּיָד חֲזָקָה וּבִזְרוֹעַ נְטוּיָה. וְאִלּוּ לֹא הוֹצִיא הַקָּדוֹשׁ בָּרוּךְ
הוּא אֶת־אֲבוֹתֵינוּ מִמִּצְרַיִם, הֲרֵי אָנוּ וּבָנֵינוּ וּבְנֵי בָנֵינוּ
מְשֻׁעְבָּדִים הָיִינוּ לְפַרְעֹה בְּמִצְרָיִם. וַאֲפִלּוּ כֻּלָּנוּ חֲכָמִים,
כֻּלָּנוּ נְבוֹנִים, כֻּלָּנוּ זְקֵנִים, כֻּלָּנוּ יוֹדְעִים אֶת־הַתּוֹרָה, מִצְוָה
עָלֵינוּ לְסַפֵּר בִּיצִיאַת מִצְרָיִם. וְכָל־הַמַּרְבֶּה לְסַפֵּר בִּיצִיאַת
מִצְרָיִם, הֲרֵי זֶה מְשֻׁבָּח.

We were slaves to Pharaoh in Mitzrayim, but Adonai our God brought us out of there with a mighty hand and an outstretched arm. Had the Holy Blessed One not taken our ancestors out of Mitzrayim, then we would still be slaves to Pharaoh in Mitzrayim—and so would our children and grandchildren. Even if we were all scholars, sages, elders, or well-versed in Torah, we would still tell the story of the Exodus from Mitzrayim. Everyone who participates in the retelling of the story deserves our attention.

Therefore, together we praise God, who was with us in Mitzrayim, who is with us tonight, and who is everywhere.

בָּרוּךְ הַמָּקוֹם. בָּרוּךְ הוּא. Barukh hamakom. Barukh hu.

בָּרוּךְ שֶׁנָּתַן תּוֹרָה Barukh shenatan torah

לְעַמּוֹ יִשְׂרָאֵל. l'amo yisra·el.

בָּרוּךְ הוּא. Barukh hu.

Praised be God who is called Hamakom. Praised be God.
Praised be God who gave the Torah to Israel. Praised be God.

What is the worst thing about being a slave to anyone?

Let My People Go

When Israel was in Egypt land,
Let my people go.
Oppressed so hard
they could not stand,
Let my people go.
Go down, Moses,
way down in Egypt land.
Tell old Pharaoh,
"Let my people go."

אַרְבָּעָה בָּנִים | **Arba'ah Banim**
The Four Children

 Each of us understands things in a different way. The Four Children represent four different responses to the seder and different levels of asking questions. So the seder contains answers to all the ways questions are asked, whether they be deep and profound or simple and straightforward. The wise child (*chakham*) is interested in knowing what you have to do to perform the seder correctly. The insensitive child (*rasha*) sees the seder as irrelevant. The uncomplicated child (*tam*) wants to know what the seder is all about—but just the basics. The young child (*she·eino yode·a lish·ol*) is eager to learn but does not yet know enough to ask.

HOW TO Taking turns, four different people should ask one question each.

What does the wise child (*chakham*) ask? "What are the specific things which Adonai asked us to do?" (Deuteronomy 6:20). Tell this child all about the laws of Pesach. This child longs to get closer to God.

What does the insensitive child (*rasha*) ask? "What does this stuff have to do with you?" (Exodus 12:26). Since this child does not feel a part of the Exodus experience, answer that the seder is done "because of what Adonai did for me when I left Mitzrayim" (Exodus 13:8). We were all there. You and I.

What does the uncomplicated child (*tam*) ask? "What happened? Just tell me the basic story." Reply: "With a mighty hand, Adonai brought us out of Mitzrayim, out of a life of slavery" (Exodus 13:14).

As for the child who does not yet know what to ask (*she·eino yode·a lish·ol*), just talk about the Exodus. Tell the whole story from start to finish. The Torah says: "You should explain to your child that we do this because of what Adonai did for me when I left Mitzrayim as a free person" (Exodus 13:8).

What other kinds of kids are there in the world? Regardless of your age, what kind of child are you?

 Imagine that you were the wisest child on earth. What advice would you give to your seder guests?

 Talk about a time when you were unable to think of a question to ask. How did you feel?

 Add a fifth child who may not be free to celebrate Passover, who asks: "Why can't we celebrate Passover with our fellow Jews?" Have everyone think of a way to help this child. Share it with the others; then go and do it.

The Ballad of the Four Sons

To the tune of "Clementine"

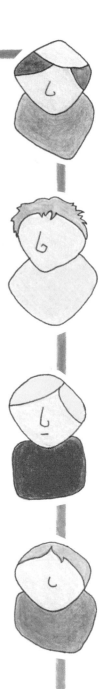

1 Said the father to his children,
"At the seder will you dine,
You will eat your fill of matzah,
You will drink four cups of wine."

2 Now this father had no daughters,
But his sons they numbered four.
One was wise and one was wicked,
One was simple and a bore.

3 And the fourth was sweet and winsome,
He was young and he was small.
While his brothers asked the questions,
He could scarcely speak at all.

4 Said the wise son to his father,
"Would you please explain the laws
Of the customs of the seder?
Will you please explain the cause?"

5 And the father proudly answered,
"As our fathers ate in speed,
Ate the Paschal lamb 'ere midnight
And from slavery were freed.

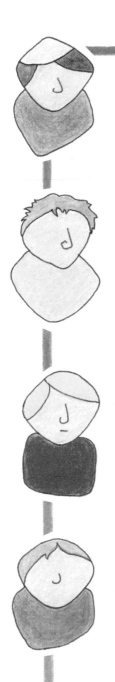

6 "So we follow their example
And 'ere midnight must complete
All the seder, and we should not
After twelve remain to eat."

7 Then did sneer the son so wicked,
"What does all this mean to you?"
And the father's voice was bitter,
And his grief and anger grew.

8 "If yourself you don't consider
As a son of Israel,
Then for you this has no meaning.
You could be a slave as well."

9 Then the simple son said simply,
"What is this?" and quietly,
The good father told his offspring,
"We were freed from slavery."

10 But the youngest child was silent,
For he could not ask at all;
His eyes were bright with wonder
As his father told him all.

11 Now, dear children, read the lesson
And remember evermore
What the father told the children,
Told his sons that numbered four.

Written by Ben Aronin.

 **The Four Children
and the Rappers**

1 Well, hey, you all! Glad you came along
To hear our story told in rhyme and song.
It's about four children and the questions
     they raise.
They think about Pesach in different ways.

2 One child is wise, one argues a lot.
One's got a brain that's not yet so hot.
One's very young and can't yet speak.
Well, now, let's take a closer peek.

3 The wise child asks, "What's the meaning
     and the cause
Of all these customs, rules, and laws?"
Since this kid understands the entire story,
The Torah says, "Tell it in all its glory!"

4 The child who argues has an attitude.
A seder just ain't for this cool dude!
A Jewish past this kid don't need.
If she'd been a slave, she'd never be freed!

5 The third child's simple. Keep your story plain.
Long explanations would be insane.
He'll just ask, "What's this?" You can then say,
"We escaped from Egypt and became free
    that day."

6 Child number four cannot be heard.
The kid's too young — doesn't speak a word.
If you waited for a question, it could take
    two years.
So begin the story for her; tell her of our hopes
    and tears.

7 Now we sure do hope you enjoyed our rap.
Did it cause you for a moment to put on your
    thinking cap?
Don't forget, though they were different,
    each daughter and son,
Kids are equally important, every one!

Adapted from an original rap created by Deborah Hercky.

וְהִיא שֶׁעָמְדָה | V'hi She·am'dah
Promises

WHY Pesach is a holiday which celebrates, among other things, the covenant between God and the Jewish people. God promised Abraham and Sarah, "Know for certain that those who come after you will be strangers in a strange land. They will be afflicted as slaves for four hundred years. But also know that I will judge that nation [Egypt] severely and they [Israel] will leave as a mighty people" (Genesis 15:13–14). In response, we recite *V'hi she·am'dah*.

HOW TO Cover the matzah and raise your cup of wine. After you have said *V'hi she·am'dah*, place your cup back on the table and uncover the matzah once again.

וְהִיא שֶׁעָמְדָה לַאֲבוֹתֵינוּ וְלָנוּ,
שֶׁלֹא אֶחָד בִּלְבַד עָמַד עָלֵינוּ לְכַלוֹתֵנוּ.
אֶלָּא שֶׁבְּכָל־דּוֹר וָדוֹר, עוֹמְדִים עָלֵינוּ לְכַלוֹתֵנוּ,
וְהַקָּדוֹשׁ בָּרוּךְ הוּא מַצִּילֵנוּ מִיָּדָם.

It is the promise to our ancestors and to us that still holds true.
Not just one enemy has arisen to destroy us.
Instead, in every generation there are people who have tried
to destroy us,
but the Holy Blessed One has saved us from their hands.

צֵא וּלְמַד | **Tzei Ulmad**
Come and Learn

WHY This part of the seder fills in the gaps in the story. We now know that the Israelites were slaves in Egypt and that God, through Moses' leadership, guided us out of Egypt. But how did we become slaves in the first place? How did Moses become such an important leader of the Jewish people? And how did Moses actually get all those people out of Egypt without being stopped by the Egyptian army? For the answers, we have to go all the way back to Joseph.

HOW TO Let's read the story together. Begin by reading the Torah text that tells it all.

אֲרַמִּי אֹבֵד אָבִי, וַיֵּרֶד מִצְרַיְמָה, וַיָּגָר שָׁם בִּמְתֵי מְעָט,
וַיְהִי־שָׁם לְגוֹי גָּדוֹל עָצוּם וָרָב.

My ancestor was a nomad from a place called Aram Naharayim. With only a few people, he went down to Mitzrayim and lived there. There my ancestor became a great nation, mighty and numerous.

וַיָּרֵעוּ אֹתָנוּ הַמִּצְרִים וַיְעַנּוּנוּ, וַיִּתְּנוּ עָלֵינוּ עֲבֹדָה קָשָׁה.

The Egyptians were cruel to us, and they forced us to work for them as slaves.

וַנִּצְעַק אֶל יי אֱלֹהֵי אֲבֹתֵינוּ, וַיִּשְׁמַע יי אֶת־קֹלֵנוּ,
וַיַּרְא אֶת־עָנְיֵנוּ וְאֶת־עֲמָלֵנוּ וְאֶת־לַחֲצֵנוּ.

We cried out to Adonai, the God of our ancestors. God heard our cry and took note of our painful life.

וַיּוֹצִאֵנוּ יי מִמִּצְרַיִם בְּיָד חֲזָקָה וּבִזְרֹעַ נְטוּיָה וּבְמֹרָא גָּדֹל,
וּבְאֹתוֹת וּבְמֹפְתִים.

So with an outstretched arm, with awesome power, and with incredible signs of divine wonder, Adonai took us out of Mitzrayim.

Deuteronomy 26:5–8

29

Hunger in the Land

There was famine in the land of Canaan, so Jacob sent his sons to get food in Egypt. Thinking that their brother Joseph was a slave (since they had sold him into slavery), they were surprised to learn that he had become the prime minister. Joseph's family joined him in Egypt, where they lived for a long time. Then Joseph died, and after several generations the Egyptian people forgot how Joseph had saved their nation from dying of starvation. It was he who had the idea to store food during good farming years so that it would be available when the farmers were not able to produce enough food for everyone. Not only did the new Pharaoh of Egypt forget what Joseph had done, but he was afraid that the Israelites were growing too strong. They had big families and were influential members of society. So the Pharaoh made them slaves.

Egyptian Slavery

But that was still not enough. Pharaoh needed a way to prevent the slaves from growing too strong, making sure that there would not be too many of them. So he cruelly decided to have all the baby Israelite boys killed at birth. This would be done by the midwives—the women who helped those who were giving birth. But two of the midwives, whose names were Shifrah and Puah, refused to do it. And the Israelite women devised ways of protecting their children.

Moses' Birthday

One woman, Yocheved, put her new son in a little straw basket and floated him down the Nile River, praying that he would be safe. She sent her daughter Miriam to look after the little boy. Meanwhile, Pharaoh's grown daughter was bathing in the river. She found the infant, adopted him, and named him Moses. Miriam ran and got her mother, who volunteered to be a wet nurse for the young boy. While tending little Moses, his natural mother Yocheved taught him the ways of the Israelites. At the same time, Pharaoh's daughter raised him as Pharaoh's grandson, a prince, a member of the Egyptian royal family.

Moses Grows Up

Moses always knew he was different. He didn't like seeing bullies beating up other people. Once, when he saw an Egyptian taskmaster whipping an Israelite slave, he couldn't stand it anymore and rescued the Israelite slave. Afraid for his own life because of what he had done, Moses fled to the desert to a place called Midian. He lived there with a shepherd named Jethro and eventually married one of Jethro's daughters, Zipporah.

One day, Moses was out tending Jethro's flock when he saw an incredible thing happen. A bush appeared to be on fire but its branches were not being burned. And he heard God speak: "Moses, take off your shoes. You are on holy ground." And God told Moses to go to Pharaoh and tell him, "Let My people go." Moses was afraid to go alone. He did not speak well. So God told Moses to take his brother Aaron with him. Moses felt God's presence, and that's what really gave him the courage to face Pharaoh and demand the release of the Israelites from slavery.

Let My People Go

Moses went to Pharaoh, who was not easy to convince. Moses demonstrated God's power, but this made Pharaoh very angry. How dare Moses make demands! And so, Pharaoh made things even worse for the Israelite slaves and made them suffer even more.

During the Magid section of the Passover seder we retell the story of our brothers and sisters in Egypt. As we retell it, imagine that you were there and fill in your own memories of the story.

A long time ago my family were slaves in Egypt. Our house in Egypt was very _____. I remember playing with _____, but most of the time I would have to go to work. When I went to work, I remember _____.

The first time I met Pharaoh I thought _____. All the kids used to say that Pharaoh would _____. One day Moses came to our people and said _____. I could hardly believe it, but I decided _____.

When the plagues finally came, I felt _____. The plague I will never forget is the one that _____. When we left Egypt, my family took three things with them. They were _____, _____, and _____.

The one thing I most remember about the matzah when we left Egypt is _____. When we reached the Red Sea, I looked at it and felt _____. When Moses raised his hand and rod and the sea split, I _____.

When we crossed the Red Sea, I felt like singing _____. All in all, I will never ever forget _____. When I have my own family, I will always make sure to tell them _____.

Place a small bucket of water on the floor and have participants jump over it to remind them of the crossing of the Red Sea.

During this section, when the Israelites finally leave Egypt, the Caucasus Mountain Jews raise their hands toward heaven and say, "May it be the will of God that the Messiah, the son of David, rescue all people in exile, as Adonai our God rescued our ancestors in times of old."

הַמַּכּוֹת | Hamakot
The Plagues

WHY Pharaoh was not persuaded by Moses' first attempt to get him to free the Israelites. And so, God wanted to show Pharaoh who he was dealing with. The plagues sound cruel, and they were. But so was the slavery the Israelites were forced to endure. Each time God brought a plague on the Egyptians, it seemed that Pharaoh was going to free the Israelites. But each time Pharaoh survived a plague, he changed his mind and made things even worse for them. Until the last plague crushed even Pharaoh's iron will.

HOW TO Read the plagues one at a time. Each time you read a plague, dip your little finger in your cup of wine and place a droplet on your plate. Don't lick your finger—these are plagues!

1	דָּם	dam	blood
2	צְפַרְדֵּעַ	tz'farde·a	frogs
3	כִּנִּים	kinim	lice
4	עָרוֹב	arov	flies
5	דֶּבֶר	dever	cattle disease
6	שְׁחִין	sh'chin	boils
7	בָּרָד	barad	hail
8	אַרְבֶּה	arbeh	locusts
9	חֹשֶׁךְ	choshekh	darkness
10	מַכַּת בְּכוֹרוֹת	makat b'khorot	death of the firstborn

Some say that Rabbi Yehudah wanted to help us remember the plagues. Others say he could not bring himself to list the plagues because of the pain they had caused the Egyptians. Remember the order of the plagues the way Rabbi Yehudah taught us.

דְּצַ"ךְ עֲדַ"שׁ בְּאַחַ"ב   D'tzakh adash b'achav

34

What are some other plagues you can think of that have created problems in our world? Go around the seder table and ask each person to share an original modern-day plague with the group. Be ready to explain why it is a plague.

Some people tilt their glasses of wine and pour out a little each time, "lessening our joy."

Use props as visual aids to enhance the plagues: for example, rubber frogs, food coloring that will turn water red, plastic insects, small foam balls for hail, and so on. Use your imagination. Be as creative as you've always wanted to be.

Here are the ten plagues in pictures. Can you name them in the proper order?

   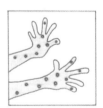

  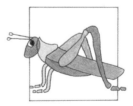 

דַּיֵּנוּ | **Dayenu**
It Would Have Been Enough

WHY Often, when we look for a way to thank God, we start singing. This well-known song expresses thanks to God for everything God did for us during the Exodus. The chorus says it all: *Dayenu*—it would have been enough. Now it's time for us to do the rest.

HOW TO Sing the three most important verses of the song. They are listed first. Don't forget the chorus.

Keep the chorus going and going and going. Then read through the remainder of the verses. Don't forget to keep the chorus going strong.

אִלּוּ הוֹצִיאָנוּ מִמִּצְרַיִם, Ilu hotzi·anu mimitz·rayim,

דַּיֵּנוּ! dayenu!

אִלּוּ נָתַן לָנוּ אֶת־הַשַּׁבָּת, Ilu natan lanu et hashabbat,

דַּיֵּנוּ! dayenu!

אִלּוּ נָתַן לָנוּ אֶת־הַתּוֹרָה, Ilu natan lanu et hatorah,

דַּיֵּנוּ! dayenu!

God brought us out of Egypt. *Dayenu!*

God punished the Egyptians and destroyed their idols. *Dayenu!*

God divided the Red Sea for us so that we could cross on dry land. *Dayenu!*

God nurtured us in the desert for forty years by feeding us heavenly manna. *Dayenu!*

God gave us Shabbat. *Dayenu!*

God brought us to Mount Sinai and gave us Torah. *Dayenu!*

God brought us to the Promised Land, to *Eretz Yisrael. Dayenu!*

God built the ancient Temple. *Dayenu!*

For each of these things and for all of them together, we sing *Dayenu!*

Dayenu means, "It would have been enough."

Some people sing *Dayenu* as a question: "Is it enough?" For example, if God had fed us manna without giving us the Shabbat, would it be enough? Here are some modern *Dayenu* questions which you may want to include in your seder:

Is it enough to give tzedakah (charity) but not personally offer to help? *Dayenu?*

Is it enough to pray and not to follow through on the values in the prayerbook? *Dayenu?*

Try to answer some modern "Is it enough?" questions.

1. Is it enough for us to read a Jewish book but not study Torah?
2. Is it enough for us to recite, "Let all who are hungry come and eat," without going out and feeding the hungry?

Fill in the blanks.
1. Is it enough for us to attend a Jewish rally without _____?
2. Is it enough for us to celebrate a seder without _____?
3. Is it enough for us to be upset with violence in the world without _____?

In some German haggadot there is a direction for the matzah balls to be thrown into the soup after the chanting of *Dayenu.*

WHY This symbol is tied to the name of the holiday. It represents the critical moment in the Passover story. After the final plague Pharaoh gave in—his own son had been killed. To prevent the plague from reaching their households, the Israelites placed blood from the spring offering on the sides and top of their doorways, covering the place where we put our mezuzot today. We point to the bone to make sure everyone remembers what happened.

HOW TO Point to the roasted bone (or red beet if you are a vegetarian) and explain what happened in your own words. Here is the way it is written in the Torah:

> You should tell them, "It is the Pesach offering to Adonai because God passed over the Israelite homes in Egypt, when the Egyptians were killed and our homes were protected."
> Exodus 12:27

בְּכָל־דּוֹר וָדוֹר | B'khol Dor Vador
In Every Generation

WHY The haggadah is not just a book of stories from the distant past. It is a living record of Jewish history, which we add to each year as we participate in the seder. We all feel part of Jewish history, from the Exodus to the giving of the Torah until today. And so, we read this section to remind ourselves of our obligation.

HOW TO Many melodies have been written for this text. Choose one you like, or just read it in a traditional chant. Sing it several times until it flows from your lips into your heart and soul.

בְּכָל־דּוֹר וָדוֹר חַיָּב אָדָם   B'khol dor vador chayav adam

לִרְאוֹת אֶת־עַצְמוֹ   lir·ot et atzmo

כְּאִלּוּ הוּא יָצָא מִמִּצְרַיִם,   k'ilu hu yatzah mimitz·rayim.

In every generation, individuals should look upon themselves as if personally freed from Mitzrayim.

Why do you think Rabban Gamliel chose pesach, matzah, and maror as the three most important symbols for the seder?

If you could choose the most important three symbols, what would they be and why?

In this part of the seder we are reminded that we must feel as if we were in Egypt and were personally freed. Imagine what it was like not to be free. Talk about what it was like to be a slave in Egypt. Share one of the first things you would have done once you were freed from the Egyptians.

When Sephardim say *B'khol dor vador*—"In every generation we must feel that we ourselves personally left Egypt"— participants pick up scallions (green onions) and beat each other on the back and shoulders. It is a reminder of the whipping that the slaves received in Egypt. Go ahead and try it.

הַלְלוּיָה | **Halleluyah**
Praise God

WHY Psalms of praise to God are recited at this point in the seder. They thank God for all of the things God did for us. The psalms in the haggadah are called the "Egyptian Hallel" because, so the rabbis tell us, these very psalms were chanted by the Israelites at the Red Sea. And that's where we are in the story.

HOW TO So let's listen to the next part of the story. But let's begin with the first two psalms from the Egyptian Hallel. The others are recited later.

Halleluyah.
Those who worship Adonai sing praises
From the rising of the sun until its setting.
May the name of Adonai be praised now and forever.

from Psalm 113

בְּצֵאת יִשְׂרָאֵל מִמִּצְרָיִם, בֵּית יַעֲקֹב מֵעַם לֹעֵז.

הָיְתָה יְהוּדָה לְקָדְשׁוֹ, יִשְׂרָאֵל מַמְשְׁלוֹתָיו.

הַיָּם רָאָה וַיָּנֹס, הַיַּרְדֵּן יִסֹּב לְאָחוֹר.

הֶהָרִים רָקְדוּ כְאֵילִים, גְּבָעוֹת כִּבְנֵי־צֹאן.

מַה־לְּךָ הַיָּם כִּי תָנוּס, הַיַּרְדֵּן תִּסֹּב לְאָחוֹר.

הֶהָרִים תִּרְקְדוּ כְאֵילִים, גְּבָעוֹת כִּבְנֵי־צֹאן.

מִלִּפְנֵי אָדוֹן חוּלִי אָרֶץ . . .

When the Israelites left Egypt, they became the holy Jewish people. During their journey, the sea washed away from the shore and the Jordan River ran backwards. Mountains looked like rams skipping. Even the earth shook. All because they felt the presence of God in their midst.

from Psalm 114

When it was finally time, the Israelites left quickly and ran toward the Red Sea. Pharaoh sent his army after them, angry at what had happened. And the Israelites were at the shore of the sea. Moses didn't know what to do. The Israelites were afraid to cross, until one man took the fateful plunge and jumped into the water. Moses raised his staff and the Red Sea parted. The Israelites crossed onto dry land. The waters returned as the Egyptian army was pursuing the Israelites—and all the soldiers were drowned.

Miriam, Moses' sister, led the Israelites in song and dance, thankful that they had been saved and were finally free.

Miriam's cup is a relatively new ritual object that some people place on the seder table beside Elijah's cup. It is filled with water and serves as a symbol of Miriam's well, which was the source of water for the Israelites in the desert. It has been said that Miriam's well followed the Israelites for forty years because of the merit of Miriam. Invite everyone at your seder table to pour some water from their drinking glasses into Miriam's cup. Then sing Miriam's song (p. 42).

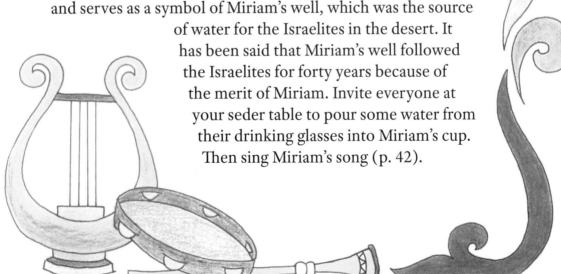

Miriam's Song

Chorus:

And the women dancing with their timbrels
Followed Miriam as she sang her song
"Sing a song to the One whom we've exalted."
Miriam and the women danced and danced the whole
    night long.

1 Miriam was a weaver of unique variety
The tapestry she wove was one which sang our history
With every strand and every thread she crafted her delight
A woman touched with spirit she dances toward the light.
Chorus

2 When Miriam stood upon the shores and gazed across the sea
The wonder of this miracle she soon came to believe
Whoever thought the sea would part with an outstretched hand
And we would pass to freedom and march to the promised land?
Chorus

3 And Miriam the prophet took the timbrel in her hand
And all the women followed her just as she
    had planned
And Miriam raised her voice in song, she sang with
    praise and might
We've just lived through a miracle, we're going to
    dance tonight.
Chorus

כּוֹס שְׁנִיָּה | Kos Sh'niyah
The Second Cup

WHY This cup of wine is for the second promise God made to our ancestors: "I will deliver you from slavery" (Exodus 6:6).

HOW TO Raise your cup while reciting the blessing. Then you may drink the second cup. Lean on your arm when drinking. Remember to get comfortable.

הִנְנִי מוּכָן וּמְזֻמָּן Hin'ni mukhan umzuman

לְקַיֵּם מִצְוַת כּוֹס שְׁנִיָּה. l'kayem mitz·vat kos sh'niyah.

I am ready to fulfill the mitzvah of drinking the second cup of wine.

בָּרוּךְ אַתָּה יי Barukh atah adonai

אֱלֹהֵינוּ מֶלֶךְ הָעוֹלָם, eloheinu melekh ha·olam,

בּוֹרֵא פְּרִי הַגָּפֶן. borei p'ri hagafen.

Praised are You, Adonai, who has freed our people.
Praised are You, Adonai our God, Guide of the Universe,
who creates the fruit that grows on the vine.

רָחְצָה | Roch·tzah
Cleansing

WHY Now we are getting ready to eat. We want to make sure that our hands are ritually clean—the same way the ancient priests cleansed their hands before preparing a sacrifice. As a holy people, we all become priests and our seder table becomes an altar. Washing is done without a blessing. Since cleansing is a ritual act, a blessing is included.

HOW TO Use a pitcher or a cup to pour water over each hand two or three times, and then recite the blessing.

בָּרוּךְ אַתָּה יי   Barukh atah adonai

אֱלֹהֵינוּ מֶלֶךְ הָעוֹלָם,   eloheinu melekh ha·olam,

אֲשֶׁר קִדְּשָׁנוּ בְּמִצְוֹתָיו,   asher kid'shanu b'mitz·votav

וְצִוָּנוּ עַל נְטִילַת יָדָיִם.   v'tzivanu al n'tilat yadayim.

Praised are You, Adonai our God, Guide of the Universe, who made us special through mitzvot and instructed us to cleanse our hands.

 Why do you think we say a blessing when we wash our hands this time? Remember, we didn't say a blessing the first time (at Ur·chatz).

מוֹצִיא מַצָּה | Motzi Matzah
Eating Matzah "Bread"

WHY Bread is a symbol for all of the things we eat on a regular basis. It is a staple of the diet in our part of the world (in other places, rice serves the same purpose). Since we are about to eat—note that our hands are ritually clean—we say a blessing of thanks to God for bread and then for the special matzah bread we are taught to eat for the week of Pesach.

HOW TO Lift the three pieces of matzah (really two and one-half pieces!) and recite the following two blessings, one for bread (which includes matzah) and one just for matzah. After you say the blessings, pass out pieces of the upper and middle matzot for eating. It's OK to eat the matzah now, but only if you are still relaxing. Don't eat the bottom piece. We have to save it for later.

בָּרוּךְ אַתָּה יי   Barukh atah adonai

אֱלֹהֵינוּ מֶלֶךְ הָעוֹלָם,   eloheinu melekh ha·olam,

הַמּוֹצִיא לֶחֶם מִן הָאָרֶץ.   hamotzi lechem min ha·aretz.

Praised are You, Adonai our God, Guide of the Universe,
who makes bread grow from the earth.

בָּרוּךְ אַתָּה יי   Barukh atah adonai

אֱלֹהֵינוּ מֶלֶךְ הָעוֹלָם,   eloheinu melekh ha·olam,

אֲשֶׁר קִדְּשָׁנוּ בְּמִצְוֹתָיו   asher kid'shanu b'mitz·votav

וְצִוָּנוּ עַל אֲכִילַת מַצָּה.   v'tzivanu al akhilat matzah.

Praised are You, Adonai our God, Guide of the Universe,
who made us special through mitzvot and instructed us to eat matzah.

What are the two earliest biblical stories that describe matzah being served? (Hint: Read Genesis, chapters 18 and 19.) Why is *hamotzi* (the blessing over bread) also said over matzah?

(Answers on page 73.)

During Passover 1944 there was no matzah in the Bergen-Belsen concentration camp. The rabbis there said that the Jewish prisoners would be allowed to eat chametz, knowing full well that if they did not, they would die of starvation. The rabbis further said that a special prayer for chametz would have to be recited. This was the prayer: "Our Father, it is known to You that it is our wish to do Your will and to celebrate Passover by eating matzah and not eating chametz. But our heart is pained because our enslavement prevents us, and we are in danger of our lives. Behold, we are ready to fulfill Your mitzvah: 'And you shall live by My laws, and not die by them.' We pray to You that You may keep us alive and redeem us soon so that we may observe Your laws and serve You with a perfect heart. Amen."

During the time of the Talmud, matzah was made with designs on it. The designs included pictures of doves, fish, and flowers.

The first matzah-making machine was invented in Austria in the late 1850s. During the Middle Ages matzot were thick, even thicker than a bagel, and circular in shape.

In New York City an estimate of the total Jewish population in 1859 was made on the basis of matzah production. Figuring an average of 5 pounds per person, it was calculated that at least 40,000 Jewish people lived in New York.

Did you know that the Egyptians were one of the first cultures to learn how to use yeast to make bread rise? Since yeast is chametz, perhaps that is why eating any yeast product on Pesach is prohibited.

מָרוֹר | Maror
Bitter Vegetable

WHY This vegetable reminds us how bitter were the lives our ancestors lived as slaves. We want to feel their pain throughout our bodies, so it's not enough just to think it, say it, or even feel it. We want to be able to actually taste their pain. The charoset we eat looks a little like the mortar the Israelite slaves used to cement bricks together when they were forced to build the Egyptian cities of Pithom and Raamses.

HOW TO Point to the maror. Dip it in the charoset. (This is the second time we dip our vegetables.) Say the blessing; then you can eat it—or at least try to eat it.

בָּרוּךְ אַתָּה יי   Barukh atah adonai

אֱלֹהֵינוּ מֶלֶךְ הָעוֹלָם,   eloheinu melekh ha·olam,

אֲשֶׁר קִדְּשָׁנוּ בְּמִצְוֹתָיו   asher kid'shanu b'mitz·votav

וְצִוָּנוּ עַל אֲכִילַת מָרוֹר.   v'tzivanu al akhilat maror.

Praised are You, Adonai our God, Guide of the Universe,
who made us special through mitzvot and instructed us to eat maror.

The word *maror* means "bitter things." Talk about all of the things that make you feel bitter. Share some solutions and ways of making bitter things sweet again.

כּוֹרֵךְ | Korekh
Hillel's Sandwich

WHY Out of respect for our great teacher Hillel, we eat this peculiar sandwich, which combines all of the ingredients of the bitterness of slavery. Hillel taught us that this is the way that people ate the Pesach (remember the roasted bone) during the time of the ancient Temple: with matzah and maror.

HOW TO Distribute pieces of the bottom matzah (the only one left from the original three). Make a sandwich of charoset and maror for each person. Just eat the sandwich. No blessing is needed because we have already said the blessings for both matzah and maror.

 The Earl of Sandwich is usually considered to be the inventor of the sandwich. Do you think that Hillel created the first sandwich when he put matzah and maror together and ate them as a sandwich almost 2,000 years ago?

Moroccan Jews grind dates and nuts into balls for charoset. Iraqi Jews make a syrup of dates. Turkish Jews add raisins and orange peel. Yemenites add grains.

שֻׁלְחָן עוֹרֵךְ | Shulchan Orekh
The Meal Is Served

WHY We begin our meal with an egg because an egg is a symbol of new life. This is the new life the Israelites enjoyed after they were freed from Egypt. Some say that we use hardboiled eggs because the more you boil an egg the harder it gets. The Israelites were the same way. The more that Pharaoh punished them, the stronger and more numerous they became.

HOW TO We know that we don't have to tell you how to eat. However, many people begin the meal with a hard-boiled egg dipped in salt water. (Since this is not a custom for all families, it's not considered a third dipping. Otherwise, we'd have to change the Four Questions!) Enjoy!

Game of Odds and Evens. Give the participants some nuts to hold in their hands. Going around the seder table, the others try to guess whether the number of nuts in a person's hand is an even or an odd number.

Initial Game. Prepare index cards with initials of Passover-related words and phrases. Ask seder participants to guess what they stand for. For example:

5 B of M   8 D of P   4 Q   4 C of W

Scrambled Words. Prepare index cards with Passover-related words with their letters scrambled. Have the seder leader hold up each card and ask participants to try to guess the word. Here are a few to get you started.

ATZMAH   NEWI   REEFMOD

(Answers on page 73.)

Seder Sentences. The seder leader reads each of the following statements, and participants fill in the blanks with their own clever answers.

a. The young chef was so new that he made matzah balls using matzah meal and _____.

b. Did you hear about the new Passover yoyo? When you throw it, it always _____.

c. Jewish scientists are working on a new food creation for Passover. It's called a matzah _____.

d. The leftover matzah balls were so hard that when you put them on a spoon, they _____.

e. They just found an ancient haggadah with a fifteenth part of the seder. It occurs at the end of the book, and it's called _____.

Broken Telephone. Prepare index cards with Passover-related sentences. The seder leader whispers the sentence to the person sitting in the next seat, and each person in turn whispers the sentence to the next person, and so on down the line. The last person then says the sentence. Try these sentences to get you started.

a. The angel of God passed over the houses of the Israelites and they were saved from death.

b. God brought us out from Egypt with a strong arm and an outstretched hand.

Ashkenazim avoid lamb as a main course at the seder because it was used as a sacrifice in the Temple. Sephardim generally eat lamb to commemorate the night of the Exodus.

צָפוּן | Tzafun
The Hidden Afikoman

WHY In order to make sure that slavery is the last thing you taste during your seder, nothing is eaten after the afikoman is shared by the participants. (But we do have two more cups of wine to go.) This assumes that you have found the afikoman, of course! The afikoman is a kind of dessert. In the days of the ancient Temple, the Pesach offering was the last thing eaten at the seder. Now that the Temple is gone, the afikoman serves as a symbol of the offering. It too is the last thing eaten at the seder. Since we are no longer hungry but we eat it anyway, it is holy eating.

HOW TO The afikoman (the piece of the middle matzah broken during Yachatz) has been hidden since early in the seder. Now go and look for it. After you have received a "finder's fee," break it into pieces and share it with everyone else.

 Why do you think that hiding and finding things are part of the Passover seder?

 The Afikoman Game. The participants sing a Passover song while the "searchers" look for the afikoman. As a searcher gets closer to the afikoman, those at the seder table sing the song more loudly. As a searcher moves away from the afikoman, sing more softly.

בָּרֵךְ | Barekh
Giving Thanks

WHY Just as we thanked God for food before we ate our meal, we now thank God after the meal with the traditional grace, Birkat Hamazon.

HOW TO If there are three people present, include the introductory section, which is an invitation to join in. With ten people, say the word *eloheinu* "God" (in parentheses) instead of "the One." We have included a short form of the prayer. Now is also the time to get ready to drink the third cup of wine, so go ahead and fill it up before you recite Birkat Hamazon.

Leader:

חֲבֵרַי, נְבָרֵךְ.   Chaverai, n'varekh.

Friends, let's give thanks.

Friends, then leader:

יְהִי שֵׁם יי מְבֹרָךְ   Y'hi shem adonai m'vorakh

מֵעַתָּה וְעַד עוֹלָם.   me·atah v'ad olam.

May Adonai be praised forever.

Leader:

בִּרְשׁוּת מָרָנָן וַחֲבֵרַי,   Birshut maranan vachaverai,

נְבָרֵךְ (אֱלֹהֵינוּ)   n'varekh (eloheinu)

שֶׁאָכַלְנוּ מִשֶּׁלוֹ.   she·akhalnu mishelo.

With your permission, my teachers and friends who are present, let's praise the One (God) whose food we have eaten.

52

Friends, then leader:

בָּרוּךְ (אֱלֹהֵינוּ)   Barukh (eloheinu)

שֶׁאָכַלְנוּ מִשֶּׁלוֹ,   she·akhalnu mishelo,

וּבְטוּבוֹ חָיִינוּ.   uvtuvo chayinu.

Praised be the One (God) whose food we have eaten and whose goodness we enjoy.

All:

בָּרוּךְ הוּא וּבָרוּךְ שְׁמוֹ.   Barukh hu uvarukh sh'mo.

Praised be Adonai, and praised be the holy name.

בָּרוּךְ אַתָּה יי   Barukh atah adonai

אֱלֹהֵינוּ מֶלֶךְ הָעוֹלָם,   eloheinu melekh ha·olam,

הַזָּן אֶת־הַכֹּל.   hazan et hakol.

Praised is Adonai our God, Guide of the Universe, who nourishes the entire world out of divine goodness and grace and with mercy. You provide food to all because Your mercy is unending.

Your goodness has caused us never to be in want for food. All this for the sake of Your great name. You provide for all. You nurture all by providing food for all the creatures You have created. Praised is Adonai, who provides food for all. Quickly build holy Jerusalem in our time. Praised be Adonai, who out of mercy rebuilds Jerusalem. I have been young and now I am old. Never have I seen the righteous so forsaken that their children are forced to beg for food. May the One who makes peace in high places make peace for us, for all the Jewish people, and for all people. Grant strength to Your people. Bless Your people with peace.

The blessing after the meal says thank you to God for our food. Talk about three other things for which you want to thank God.

כּוֹס שְׁלִישִׁית | Kos Sh'lishit
The Third Cup

WHY This time we drink wine to remember the third of God's promises to bring us out of Egypt: "I will rescue you with an outstretched arm and incredible decisions" (Exodus 6:6).

HOW TO Lift up your cup, and recite the blessing. Then, while still leaning on your side, drink your third cup.

הִנְנִי מוּכָן וּמְזֻמָּן   Hin'ni mukhan umzuman

לְקַיֵּם מִצְוַת כּוֹס שְׁלִישִׁית.   l'kayem mitz·vat kos sh'lishit.

I am ready to fulfill the mitzvah of drinking the third cup of wine.

בָּרוּךְ אַתָּה יי   Barukh atah adonai

אֱלֹהֵינוּ מֶלֶךְ הָעוֹלָם,   eloheinu melekh ha·olam,

בּוֹרֵא פְּרִי הַגָּפֶן.   borei p'ri hagafen.

Praised are You, Adonai our God, Guide of the Universe, who creates the fruit that grows on the vine.

אֵלִיָּהוּ הַנָּבִיא | **Eliyahu Hanavi**
Welcoming Elijah the Prophet

WHY According to Jewish tradition, Elijah the Prophet is the one who will announce that the messianic era is coming. It's a big word for a big time! Since the seder is a time when we celebrate freedom and liberty, we wait and hope for Elijah to come and announce the ultimate in freedom and liberty.

HOW TO Fill Elijah's cup. Some people do it by adding a little wine from their own cups as they fill their cups now to prepare for the fourth cup (which we will drink later). Send someone to open the front door while you read the following passages. Don't forget to close the door afterwards!

שְׁפֹךְ חֲמָתְךָ אֶל הַגּוֹיִם אֲשֶׁר לֹא יְדָעוּךָ,

וְעַל מַמְלָכוֹת אֲשֶׁר בְּשִׁמְךָ לֹא קָרָאוּ.

כִּי אָכַל אֶת־יַעֲקֹב, וְאֶת־נָוֵהוּ הֵשַׁמּוּ.

Pour out Your anger on those who do not know You, on all those governments that do not cry out to You. They have destroyed the dwelling place of the people of Jacob, now called Israel.

Psalm 79:6–7

אֵלִיָּהוּ הַנָּבִיא, אֵלִיָּהוּ הַתִּשְׁבִּי,   Eliyahu hanavi, eliyahu hatishbi,

אֵלִיָּהוּ, אֵלִיָּהוּ, אֵלִיָּהוּ הַגִּלְעָדִי.   Eliyahu, eliyahu, eliyahu hagil·adi.

בִּמְהֵרָה בְיָמֵינוּ יָבוֹא אֵלֵינוּ   Bimherah v'yameinu yavo eleinu

עִם מָשִׁיחַ בֶּן דָּוִד,   im mashiach ben david,

עִם מָשִׁיחַ בֶּן דָּוִד.   im mashiach ben david.

May Elijah the Prophet come quickly in our day and bring the time of the Messiah.

How can you help God feed the world? What will the world look like when the Messiah comes?

Pass around Elijah's cup and have all the participants at your seder pour some of their wine into it, symbolizing cooperation toward working for peace.

Have someone dress up as Elijah and wait outside at the door.

Yemenite Jews do not use Elijah's cup.

הַלֵּל | Hallel
Songs of Praise

WHY The word *hallel* means "praise." It is the name for a group of psalms (113–118) that the Levites sang in the ancient Jerusalem Temple. The Hallel psalms all thank God for the many things God has done for the Jewish people. We recited two of the Hallel psalms before the meal (p. 40). Now we say the rest of them. We divide the Hallel so that we can include the meal as part of our way of singing praise to God.

HOW TO This section concludes with the drinking of the fourth cup. Some people include songs at this time in the seder also, after Hallel, before the fourth cup.

> Adonai remembers us with blessing.
> God will bless the house of Israel.
> God will bless the house of Aaron.
> Blessed are you who honor Adonai, both the young and the old.
> May Adonai send you and your children blessings.
> May you be blessed by Adonai, the One who creates heaven
> and earth.
> The heavens are the heavens of Adonai, but the earth was given
> to humans.
> The dead cannot sing, "Halleluyah."
> Those who are silent cannot praise God.
> So we praise God now and forever.
> Halleluyah.
>
> from Psalm 115

הַלְלוּ אֶת יי כָּל־גּוֹיִם, שַׁבְּחוּהוּ כָּל־הָאֻמִּים.
כִּי גָבַר עָלֵינוּ חַסְדּוֹ, וֶאֱמֶת יי לְעוֹלָם. הַלְלוּיָהּ.

Praise Adonai, all you nations; praise God, all you peoples.
For God's acts of kindness are great, and the truth of Adonai
is forever. Halleluyah.

from Psalm 117

הוֹדוּ לַיי כִּי טוֹב,	Hodu ladonai ki tov,
כִּי לְעוֹלָם חַסְדּוֹ.	ki l'olam chasdo.
יֹאמַר נָא יִשְׂרָאֵל,	Yomar na yisra·el,
כִּי לְעוֹלָם חַסְדּוֹ.	ki l'olam chasdo.
יֹאמְרוּ נָא בֵית אַהֲרֹן,	Yom'ru na veit aharon,
כִּי לְעוֹלָם חַסְדּוֹ.	ki l'olam chasdo.
יֹאמְרוּ נָא יִרְאֵי יי,	Yom'ru na yir·ei adonai,
כִּי לְעוֹלָם חַסְדּוֹ.	ki l'olam chasdo.

Give thanks to Adonai, for all is good—
God's kindness is forever.

Israel should say:
God's kindness is forever.

The House of Aaron should say:
God's kindness is forever.

Everyone who reveres God should say:
God's kindness is forever.

from Psalm 118

God has many different names, and each one tells us
something special about God. Fill in the blanks:

God is called a Rock because _____.

God is called our Parent because _____.

God is called our Shepherd because _____.

58

נִשְׁמַת כָּל־חַי | **Nishmat Kol Chai**
All Living Things

WHY This songlike prayer is said every Shabbat and holiday in the synagogue. It is really an expression of hope that one day everyone on earth will believe in the One God of all creation.

HOW TO Just join together in prayer! Following *Nishmat kol chai*, before the fourth cup, many families sing here, as well.

נִשְׁמַת כָּל־חַי תְּבָרֵךְ אֶת־שִׁמְךָ, יי אֱלֹהֵינוּ.

וְרוּחַ כָּל־בָּשָׂר תְּפָאֵר וּתְרוֹמֵם זִכְרְךָ מַלְכֵּנוּ תָּמִיד.

מִן הָעוֹלָם וְעַד הָעוֹלָם אַתָּה אֵל,

וּמִבַּלְעָדֶיךָ אֵין לָנוּ מֶלֶךְ גּוֹאֵל וּמוֹשִׁיעַ,

פּוֹדֶה וּמַצִּיל וּמְפַרְנֵס וּמְרַחֵם, בְּכָל־עֵת צָרָה וְצוּקָה.

אֵין לָנוּ מֶלֶךְ אֶלָּא־אָתָּה,

אֱלֹהֵי הָרִאשׁוֹנִים וְהָאַחֲרוֹנִים, אֱלוֹהַּ כָּל־בְּרִיּוֹת,

אֲדוֹן כָּל־תּוֹלָדוֹת, הַמְהֻלָּל בְּרֹב הַתִּשְׁבָּחוֹת,

הַמְנַהֵג עוֹלָמוֹ בְּחֶסֶד וּבְרִיּוֹתָיו בְּרַחֲמִים.

וַיי לֹא יָנוּם וְלֹא יִישָׁן,

הַמְעוֹרֵר יְשֵׁנִים וְהַמֵּקִיץ נִרְדָּמִים, וְהַמֵּשִׂיחַ אִלְּמִים,

וְהַמַּתִּיר אֲסוּרִים, וְהַסּוֹמֵךְ נוֹפְלִים, וְהַזּוֹקֵף כְּפוּפִים,

לְךָ לְבַדְּךָ אֲנַחְנוּ מוֹדִים.

Everything that lives praises You, Adonai our God. Everything that breathes seeks Your divine guidance. For all time, You are God. No one but You is able to rescue or redeem us, to save us and nurture us, to show us mercy in times of disaster. God of all times and all living things, You guide the world with divine kindness and compassion. You who do not sleep or rest, awake the sleeping, support those who are falling, free those who are in shackles, raise those hunched over, and provide speech for those who cannot talk. Only You do we recognize as God.

מִמִּצְרַיִם גְּאַלְתָּנוּ יי אֱלֹהֵינוּ, וּמִבֵּית עֲבָדִים פְּדִיתָנוּ.
בְּרָעָב זַנְתָּנוּ וּבְשָׂבָע כִּלְכַּלְתָּנוּ,
מֵחֶרֶב הִצַּלְתָּנוּ וּמִדֶּבֶר מִלַּטְתָּנוּ,
וּמֵחֳלָיִם רָעִים וְנֶאֱמָנִים דִּלִּיתָנוּ.
עַד הֵנָּה עֲזָרוּנוּ רַחֲמֶיךָ, וְלֹא עֲזָבוּנוּ חֲסָדֶיךָ,
וְאַל תִּטְּשֵׁנוּ יי אֱלֹהֵינוּ לָנֶצַח.

From Mitzrayim, You rescued us. From a life of slavery You freed us. When we were hungry, You fed us and continued to sustain us. You saved us from death and protected us from disease. To this day, Your compassion continues to help us. You have never neglected us. Please, God, never abandon us.

כּוֹס רְבִיעִית | **Kos R'vi·it**
The Fourth Cup

WHY   Some scholars believe that it was the experience of the Exodus that actually made the Jews into a people. We drink our concluding cup of wine with the final promise: "I will take you to be My people, and I will be your God" (Exodus 6:7).

HOW TO   Raise your fourth cup of wine. Drink it—still relaxing— after you have said the blessing.

הִנְנִי מוּכָן וּמְזֻמָּן   Hin'ni mukhan umzuman

לְקַיֵּם מִצְוַת כּוֹס רְבִיעִית.   l'kayem mitz·vat kos r'vi·it.

I am ready to fulfill the mitzvah of drinking the fourth cup of wine.

בָּרוּךְ אַתָּה יי   Barukh atah adonai

אֱלֹהֵינוּ מֶלֶךְ הָעוֹלָם,   eloheinu melekh ha·olam,

בּוֹרֵא פְּרִי הַגָּפֶן.   borei p'ri hagafen.

Praised are You, Adonai our God, Guide of the Universe, who creates the fruit that grows on the vine.

After drinking the wine, say this blessing in gratitude for God's gift of wine to drink.

On Shabbat add the words in brackets.

בָּרוּךְ אַתָּה יי אֱלֹהֵינוּ מֶלֶךְ הָעוֹלָם, עַל הַגֶּפֶן וְעַל פְּרִי
הַגֶּפֶן, וְעַל תְּנוּבַת הַשָּׂדֶה, וְעַל אֶרֶץ חֶמְדָּה טוֹבָה וּרְחָבָה,
שֶׁרָצִיתָ וְהִנְחַלְתָּ לַאֲבוֹתֵינוּ לֶאֱכֹל מִפִּרְיָהּ וְלִשְׂבֹּעַ מִטּוּבָהּ.
רַחֵם יי אֱלֹהֵינוּ עַל יִשְׂרָאֵל עַמֶּךָ, וְעַל יְרוּשָׁלַיִם עִירֶךָ,
וְעַל צִיּוֹן מִשְׁכַּן כְּבוֹדֶךָ, וְעַל מִזְבַּחֶךָ וְעַל הֵיכָלֶךָ. וּבְנֵה
יְרוּשָׁלַיִם עִיר הַקֹּדֶשׁ בִּמְהֵרָה בְיָמֵינוּ, וְהַעֲלֵנוּ לְתוֹכָהּ
וְשַׂמְּחֵנוּ בְּבִנְיָנָהּ, וְנֹאכַל מִפִּרְיָהּ וְנִשְׂבַּע מִטּוּבָהּ, וּנְבָרֶכְךָ
עָלֶיהָ בִּקְדֻשָּׁה וּבְטָהֳרָה [וּרְצֵה וְהַחֲלִיצֵנוּ בְּיוֹם הַשַּׁבָּת הַזֶּה],
וְשַׂמְּחֵנוּ בְּיוֹם חַג הַמַּצּוֹת הַזֶּה. כִּי אַתָּה יי טוֹב וּמֵיטִיב
לַכֹּל, וְנוֹדֶה לְךָ עַל הָאָרֶץ וְעַל פְּרִי הַגֶּפֶן. בָּרוּךְ אַתָּה יי,
עַל הָאָרֶץ וְעַל פְּרִי הַגֶּפֶן.

Praised are You, Adonai our God, Guide of the Universe, for the vine and its fruit. We thank You for all of earth's produce and for the land that You gave our ancestors. Adonai, our God, have mercy on Your people, on Your holy city of Jerusalem, on Zion where You dwell, and on the ancient Temple. Build the holy city of Jerusalem quickly while we are all still alive, so that we may celebrate its rebuilding, eat of its produce, and praise You. Give us all [rest on this Shabbat and] joy on this Pesach. We thank You, God, for the goodness You give to all. We thank You for the land and the fruit that grows on the vine. Praised are You, Adonai our God, for the land and for the fruit that grows on the vine.

נִרְצָה | Nir·tzah
Acceptance

WHY Now we are at the end of the seder, and we ask God to accept the gifts of thoughts and feelings that we have offered. We are grateful to be free and want to show our gratitude!

HOW TO This is the easy part. Our stomachs are full and we may be a little sleepy. But there is always room for a song. So after reading the passage below, sing all of your favorite Passover songs.

חֲסַל סִדּוּר פֶּסַח כְּהִלְכָתוֹ, כְּכָל־מִשְׁפָּטוֹ וְחֻקָּתוֹ.
כַּאֲשֶׁר זָכִינוּ לְסַדֵּר אוֹתוֹ, כֵּן נִזְכֶּה לַעֲשׂוֹתוֹ.
זָךְ שׁוֹכֵן מְעוֹנָה, קוֹמֵם קְהַל עֲדַת מִי מָנָה.
בְּקָרוֹב נַהֵל נִטְעֵי כַנָּה, פְּדוּיִים לְצִיּוֹן בְּרִנָּה.

Our seder is now complete, according to Jewish custom and law. Just as we have celebrated it this year, may we together celebrate it in years to come. With our people we have gone from Mitzrayim to Israel. As we have stood as witnesses to Your covenant, may You continue to redeem us in Zion as you have promised.

לְשָׁנָה הַבָּאָה **Lashanah haba·ah**
בִּירוּשָׁלָיִם! **birushalayim!**

May we celebrate together
as a free people
next year in Jerusalem!

Use your imagination and talk about the seder now that it is over. How did you feel about it before? How do you feel about it now? What are some of your thoughts for the future?

My most important memory of this seder will be
_____.

My favorite part of this seder was _____.

The funniest thing that happened at this seder was
_____.

For next year's seder I hope _____.

Seder Songs

אַדִּיר הוּא | Adir Hu
God Is Mighty

1 אַדִּיר הוּא, אַדִּיר הוּא

Adir hu, adir hu

יִבְנֶה בֵיתוֹ בְּקָרוֹב
בִּמְהֵרָה, בִּמְהֵרָה
בְּיָמֵינוּ, בְּקָרוֹב
אֵל בְּנֵה, אֵל בְּנֵה
בְּנֵה בֵיתְךָ בְּקָרוֹב.

Yivneh veito b'karov
bimherah, bimherah
b'yameinu b'karov
el b'neh, el b'neh
b'neh veit'kha b'karov.

2 בָּחוּר הוּא, גָּדוֹל הוּא,
דָּגוּל הוּא, יִבְנֶה בֵּיתוֹ . . .

Bachur hu, gadol hu,
dagul hu, yivneh veito . . .

3 הָדוּר הוּא, וָתִיק הוּא,
זַכַּאי הוּא, יִבְנֶה בֵּיתוֹ . . .

Hadur hu, vatik hu,
zakai hu, yivneh veito . . .

4 חָסִיד הוּא, טָהוֹר הוּא,
יָחִיד הוּא, יִבְנֶה בֵּיתוֹ . . .

Chasid hu, tahor hu,
yachid hu, yivneh veito . . .

5 כַּבִּיר הוּא, לָמוּד הוּא,
מֶלֶךְ הוּא, יִבְנֶה בֵּיתוֹ . . .

Kabir hu, lamud hu,
melekh hu, yivneh veito . . .

6 נוֹרָא הוּא, סַגִּיב הוּא,
עִזּוּז הוּא, יִבְנֶה בֵּיתוֹ . . .

Norah hu, sagiv hu,
izuz hu, yivneh veito . . .

7 פּוֹדֶה הוּא, צַדִּיק הוּא,
קָדוֹשׁ הוּא, יִבְנֶה בֵּיתוֹ . . .

Podeh hu, tzadik hu,
kadosh hu, yivneh veito . . .

8 רַחוּם הוּא, שַׁדַּי הוּא,
תַּקִּיף הוּא, יִבְנֶה בֵּיתוֹ . . .

Rachum hu, shadai hu,
takif hu, yivneh veito . . .

אֶחָד מִי יוֹדֵעַ | Echad Mi Yode·a
Who Knows One?

1 Who knows **one**? I know **one**.
 One is our God in heaven and on earth.

2 Who knows **two**? I know **two**.
Two are the tablets of the covenant.
One is our God in heaven and on earth.

3 Who knows **three**? I know **three**.
Three are the patriarchs.
Two are the tablets of the covenant.
One is our God in heaven and on earth.

4 Who knows **four**? I know **four**.
Four are the matriarchs.
Three are the patriarchs.
Two are the tablets of the covenant.
One is our God in heaven and on earth.

5 Who knows **five**? I know **five**.
Five are the books of the Torah.
Four are the matriarchs.
Three are the patriarchs.
Two are the tablets of the covenant.
One is our God in heaven and on earth.

6 Who knows **six**? I know **six**.
Six are the sections of the Mishnah.
Five are the books of the Torah.
Four are the matriarchs.
Three are the patriarchs.
Two are the tablets of the covenant.
One is our God in heaven and on earth.

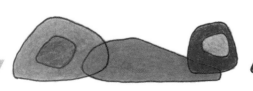

7 Who knows **seven**? I know **seven**.
Seven are the days of the week.
Six are the sections of the Mishnah.
Five are the books of the Torah.
Four are the matriarchs.
Three are the patriarchs.
Two are the tablets of the covenant.
One is our God in heaven and on earth.

8 Who knows **eight**? I know **eight**.
Eight are the days to circumcision.
Seven are the days of the week.
Six are the sections of the Mishnah.
Five are the books of the Torah.
Four are the matriarchs.
Three are the patriarchs.
Two are the tablets of the covenant.
One is our God in heaven and on earth.

9 Who knows **nine**? I know **nine**.
Nine are the months of childbirth.
Eight are the days to circumcision.
Seven are the days of the week.
Six are the sections of the Mishnah.
Five are the books of the Torah.
Four are the matriarchs.
Three are the patriarchs.
Two are the tablets of the covenant.
One is our God in heaven and on earth.

10 Who knows **ten**? I know **ten**.
Ten are the commandments from Sinai.
Nine are the months of childbirth.
Eight are the days to circumcision.
Seven are the days of the week.
Six are the sections of the Mishnah.
Five are the books of the Torah.
Four are the matriarchs.
Three are the patriarchs.
Two are the tablets of the covenant.
One is our God in heaven and on earth.

11 Who knows **eleven**? I know **eleven**.
Eleven are the stars in Joseph's dream.
Ten are the commandments from Sinai.
Nine are the months of childbirth.
Eight are the days to circumcision.
Seven are the days of the week.
Six are the sections of the Mishnah.
Five are the books of the Torah.
Four are the matriarchs.
Three are the patriarchs.
Two are the tablets of the covenant.
One is our God in heaven and on earth.

12 Who knows twelve? I know twelve.
Twelve are the tribes of Israel.
Eleven are the stars in Joseph's dream.
Ten are the commandments from Sinai.
Nine are the months of childbirth.
Eight are the days to circumcision.
Seven are the days of the week.
Six are the sections of the Mishnah.
Five are the books of the Torah.
Four are the matriarchs.
Three are the patriarchs.
Two are the tablets of the covenant.
One is our God in heaven and on earth.

13 Who knows **thirteen**? I know **thirteen**.
Thirteen are the attributes of God.
Twelve are the tribes of Israel.
Eleven are the stars in Joseph's dream.
Ten are the commandments from Sinai.
Nine are the months of childbirth.
Eight are the days to circumcision.
Seven are the days of the week.
Six are the sections of the Mishnah.
Five are the books of the Torah.
Four are the matriarchs.
Three are the patriarchs.
Two are the tablets of the covenant.
One is our God in heaven and on earth.

Here is a game you will enjoy playing. The first two columns give the verses of *Echad Mi Yode·a* as they appear in the haggadah. For the right-hand column, think of your own song verse related to the number, and share it with the other participants at your seder.

Who knows...?	I know...	I also know...
One	One is our God in heaven and on earth.	One is . . .
Two	Two are the tablets of the covenant.	Two are . . .
Three	Three are the patriarchs.	Three are . . .
Four	Four are the matriarchs.	Four are . . .
Five	Five are the books of the Torah.	Five are . . .
Six	Six are the sections of the Mishnah.	Six are . . .
Seven	Seven are the days of the week.	Seven are . . .
Eight	Eight are the days to circumcision.	Eight are . . .
Nine	Nine are the months to childbirth.	Nine are . . .
Ten	Ten are the commandments from Sinai.	Ten are . . .
Eleven	Eleven are the stars in Joseph's dream.	Eleven are . . .
Twelve	Twelve are the tribes of Israel.	Twelve are . . .
Thirteen	Thirteen are the attributes of God.	Thirteen are . . .

חַד גַּדְיָא | Chad Gadya
Just One Kid

1 One kid, just one kid.
My father bought for two zuzim,
one kid, just one kid.
Chad gadya, chad gadya.

2 Then came a cat and ate the kid
that my father bought for two zuzim.
Chad gadya, chad gadya.

3 Then came a dog and bit the cat
that ate the kid
that my father bought for two zuzim.
Chad gadya, chad gadya.

4 Then came a stick and beat the dog
that bit the cat that ate the kid
that my father bought for two zuzim.
Chad gadya, chad gadya.

5 Then came a fire and burned the stick
that beat the dog
that bit the cat that ate the kid
that my father bought for two zuzim.
Chad gadya, chad gadya.

6 Then came water and quenched the fire
that burned the stick that beat the dog
that bit the cat that ate the kid
that my father bought for two zuzim.
Chad gadya, chad gadya.

7   Then came an ox and drank the water
that quenched the fire
that burned the stick that beat the dog
that bit the cat that ate the kid
that my father bought for two zuzim.
Chad gadya, chad gadya.

8   Then came a shochet who slaughtered the ox
that drank the water that quenched the fire
that burned the stick that beat the dog
that bit the cat that ate the kid
that my father bought for two zuzim.
Chad gadya, chad gadya.

9   Then came the angel of death
who killed the shochet who slaughtered the ox
that drank the water that quenched the fire
that burned the stick that beat the dog
that bit the cat that ate the kid
that my father bought for two zuzim.
Chad gadya, chad gadya.

10   Then came the Holy One
who killed the angel of death
who killed the shochet who slaughtered the ox
that drank the water that quenched the fire
that burned the stick that beat the dog
that bit the cat that ate the kid
that my father bought for two zuzim.
Chad gadya, chad gadya.

Create a sound for each character or object in the story of *Chad Gadya.* As you sing the song and a character or object is mentioned, make the sound for that character. For example, when the cat is mentioned, someone says, "Meow." When the dog is mentioned someone says, "Bow wow," and so on.

Going around the table, have each person at your seder sing a different verse of *Chad Gadya.* See if each person can sing the verse in one breath!

Chad Gadya has been explained as a story describing Israel's trials with its enemies throughout history. Everything mentioned in the song is a symbol. The kid represents Israel, and the father is God, the Holy One. The *zuzim* are the two tablets of the law, and the remaining figures are Israel's enemies: Assyria (the cat), Babylon (the dog), Persia (the stick), Greece (the fire), Rome (the water), the Saracens (the ox), the Crusaders (the slaughterer), and the Ottoman Turks (the angel of death).

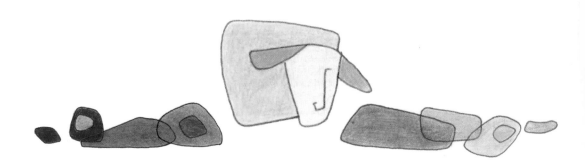

כִּי לוֹ נָאֶה | Ki Lo Na·eh

To You, Only to You

1 אַדִּיר בִּמְלוּכָה,
בָּחוּר כַּהֲלָכָה,
גְּדוּדָיו יֹאמְרוּ לוֹ:
לְךָ וּלְךָ, לְךָ כִּי לְךָ,
לְךָ אַף לְךָ,
לְךָ יי הַמַּמְלָכָה,
כִּי לוֹ נָאֶה, כִּי לוֹ יָאֶה.

Adir bimlukhah,
bachur kahalakhah,
g'dudav yom'ru lo:
L'kha ul·kha, l'kha ki l'kha,
l'kha af l'kha,
l'kha adonai hamamlakhah,
ki lo na·eh, ki lo ya·eh.

2 דָּגוּל בִּמְלוּכָה,
הָדוּר כַּהֲלָכָה,
וָתִיקָיו יֹאמְרוּ לוֹ: לְךָ וּלְךָ ...

Dagul bimlukhah,
hadur kahalakhah,
vatikav yom'ru lo: L'kha ul·kha ...

3 זַכַּאי בִּמְלוּכָה,
חָסִין כַּהֲלָכָה,
טַפְסְרָיו יֹאמְרוּ לוֹ: לְךָ וּלְךָ ...

Zakai bimlukhah,
chasin kahalakhah,
taf·s'rav yom'ru lo: L'kha ul·kha ...

4 יָחִיד בִּמְלוּכָה,
כַּבִּיר כַּהֲלָכָה,
לִמּוּדָיו יֹאמְרוּ לוֹ: לְךָ וּלְךָ ...

Yachid bimlukhah,
kabir kahalakhah,
limudav yom'ru lo: L'kha ul·kha ...

5 מוֹשֵׁל בִּמְלוּכָה,
נוֹרָא כַּהֲלָכָה,
סְבִיבָיו יֹאמְרוּ לוֹ: לְךָ וּלְךָ ...

Moshel bimlukhah,
norah kahalakhah,
s'vivav yom'ru lo: L'kha ul·kha ...

6 עָנָו בִּמְלוּכָה,
פּוֹדֶה כַּהֲלָכָה,
צַדִּיקָיו יֹאמְרוּ לוֹ: לְךָ וּלְךָ ...

Anav bimlukhah,
podeh kahalakhah,
tzadikav yom'ru lo: L'kha ul·kha ...

7 קָדוֹשׁ בִּמְלוּכָה,
רַחוּם כַּהֲלָכָה,
שִׁנְאַנָּיו יֹאמְרוּ לוֹ: לְךָ וּלְךָ ...

Kadosh bimlukhah,
rachum kahalakhah,
shin·anav yom'ru lo: L'kha ul·kha ...

8 תַּקִּיף בִּמְלוּכָה,
תּוֹמֵךְ כַּהֲלָכָה,
תְּמִימָיו יֹאמְרוּ לוֹ: לְךָ וּלְךָ ...

Takif bimlukhah,
tomekh kahalakhah,
t'mimav yom'ru lo: L'kha ul·kha ...

Answers

Page 10

MATZAH   EGYPT   WATER   SALT   KID

Page 19

The Four Questions are not answered immediately because we must first read about slavery in the haggadah and remember when we were slaves in Egypt. Then we can talk about being free people.

Page 44

This washing precedes the blessing over matzah, which officially begins the meal. We always say a blessing before beginning the actual meal.

Page 46

Abraham served matzah to the three angel visitors. (Genesis 18) Lot served matzah to the two angels who visited him at Sodom. (Genesis 19)

Matzah, although it did not rise, is still bread. We say the blessing *hamotzi* whenever we eat any kind of bread.

Page 49

Initial Game

5 Books of Moses   8 Days of Passover   4 Questions   4 Cups of Wine

Scrambled Words

MATZAH   WINE   FREEDOM

Glos[sary]

Aram Naharyaim Often used interchangea[bly] [with] and Haran, it is the place where Abraham lives with his father's family after leaving the city of Ur.

Babylonian Talmud The first source book of Jewish law, with over 2,000 scholarly contributors. It is composed of the Mishnah, edited by Judah the Prince (200 C.E.), and the Gemara, which explains the Mishnah, completed in approximately 500 C.E.

Bukharan Jews Jews of Central Asia who are said to have traced their ancestry to the tribes of both Issachar and Naphtali.

Canaan Name for the territory in biblical times that was principally in Phoenicia. It is the land that God promises to Abraham (Genesis 12:17).

Caucasus Mountain Jews Jews of the eastern and northern slopes of Caucasus. They originated from ancient Persia and settled in remote mountainous areas.

Earl of Sandwich An eighteenth-century British statesman, John Montagu, the fourth Earl of Sandwich, who is best known for the claim that he was the inventor of the sandwich.

Elijah the Prophet Prophet in the kingdom of Israel (9th century B.C.E.) known for his opposition to idol worship.

Gematria Using the number values of Hebrew letters to determine the meanings of words.

Haggadot Plural of *haggadah,* literally "the telling (of the story)."

Kabbalist A Jewish mystic, a person seeking direct knowledge of God using meditation and prayer.

Kohen The Jewish priest, traditionally considered to be directly descended from Aaron.

Levi The biblical tribe that received no allotment of land in ancient Israel because it was set apart to conduct the worship of God.

Matriarchs Sarah, Rebekah, Rachel, and Leah, the founding mothers of the Israelites.

Messiah Literally meaning "one who is anointed," he is described in the books of the Jewish prophets as a divinely appointed ideal ruler (descended from King David) who leads the world in righteousness and peace.

Midwife A person trained to assist a woman in childbirth.

Mishnah Legal codification that expands our understanding of the Bible, compiled and edited by Judah the Prince (200 C.E.).

Moroccan Jews Jews who live in and around the North African country of Morocco. They first migrated to this area after the destruction of the Second Temple in Jerusalem.

Nisan The first month of the Hebrew calendar, which includes Passover.

Patriarchs Abraham, Isaac, and Jacob, the founding fathers of the Jewish people.

Rabban Gamliel President of the ancient court known as the Sanhedrin; grandson of Rabbi Hillel.

Sedarim Plural of *seder,* the table ceremony held on the first two nights of Passover. The seder celebrates the holiday and retells the Exodus using the Haggadah. In Reform practice, generally only a first seder is held.

Sephardic Jews Descendants of the Jews of Spain, the Sephardim arrived in Palestine in the fifteenth century after their expulsion from Spain.

Yemenite Jews Jews from Yemen, a Moslem state in the Middle East. The first Yemenites arrived in Palestine in the sixteenth century.

Zuzim Plural of *zuz,* an ancient Jewish silver coin struck during the Bar Kochba revolt (132–136 C.E.).